HD
9999
.C72
A3
N5

B  897,926

# Behind the Scenes
## in Candy Factories

*Published—March, 1928—by*

## The Consumers' League of New York
### 289 Fourth Avenue
### New York City

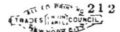

*This study is the second of those made possible by the Alice Day Jackson Fund as a memorial to Mrs. Jackson's work during her five years as President of the Consumers' League of New York, 1921 to 1926.*

*The Chocolate Dipper*   By Ewing Galloway, N. Y.

## FOREWORD

THE manager of one of the city's largest candy factories remarked during the course of this investigation, "The less the public knows about candy making the better."

It has been the function of the Consumers' League of New York during the thirty-seven years of its existence to acquaint the consuming public with the conditions under which the things they eat, wear and use are made and sold. This candy study was made for that purpose.

The candy industry in New York City was chosen for this investigation because of the fact that in the five great women employing industries studied by the New York State Bureau of Women in Industry in 1923 (Bulletin 121, Department of Labor), the women candy-makers had the lowest scale of earnings.

There is at this time a wide-spread belief that any willing worker, even though a woman and unskilled, can, if she will, earn enough to support herself in health and decency. The current acceptance of this is probably due to a superficial comparison of today's wage scales with the "sweated-wage" of twenty years ago which shows a considerable increase even for the unskilled worker. A comparison of cost-of-living figures, however, and a consideration of the long periods of unemployment or partial employment in seasonal industries, shows that many women in the City of New York earn less than the wage computed by the most conservative organizations as a fair minimum. That the majority of these low-wage workers are young girls who live at home with their families and are partially supported by those families, explains but does not alter this fact. Very often they come from families of unskilled laborers where there is no legitimate margin with which to carry them.

Nevertheless, this report is not offered primarily as a wage study because the Consumers' League, being an unofficial organization, has no power to demand access to payrolls. The wage problem is covered, however, both through the personal experience of the investigators, and by the findings of the State Department of Labor taken from actual payrolls.

While only twenty-five candy factories in New York City were actually worked in by the investigators, an attempt was made to cover a typical cross-section of the industry, from the little loft factory in the dirty side street turning out the cheapest grade of lollipop, to the large model daylight factory whose products are nationally advertised. That some of the best as well as some of the worst examples in the industry were missed, is quite possible. That the investigator, and those who assisted her, working as beginners for the most part, came in contact with the unskilled and badly paid section of the workers, is also true. But this unskilled group is the largest and most representative class of candy workers and information gained by this working contact was supplemented by interviews with more highly skilled workers, with employers and managers.

While wages are perhaps the most vital of statistics to the woman candy maker, sanitation focuses the attention of the consumer of candy. Do the conditions under which candy is made also approach a reasonable "health and decency standard"? Can such a standard both of working conditions and sanitation, be maintained without imposing too great a financial burden on the industry or the community? The answer seems to be that it can since even among the limited number studied a few plants have achieved these requirements.

The following study is presented as a picture of a low-wage industry in relation to the women who do its work and to the public who consumes its product.

—Frances Perkins.

## A WEEK IN A CANDY FACTORY.*

Long before eight the line of job-hunters began gathering at ..........'s in answer to the advertisement for both experienced and inexperienced candy workers. The middle-aged women were the first to arrive and the most determined. There were no benches or chairs, so we stood about, first on one foot, then on the other, or tried to edge around near the wall so we could lean against it. Within half an hour there were sixty or seventy women crowded into the tiny hall. Latecomers, those arriving after 8:30, were not able to get inside. Most of the girls were young, in their early teens, it seemed, but the few older ones were around fifty. Italian girls predominated with a scattering of Polish and Irish. Two girls were Porto Rican and spoke no word of English. One of them was strikingly beautiful. Among the older women was one I had met the week before looking for another job. She was in her fifties and unmarried and she told me she was being turned down everywhere because of her age. She was a pale, frail little thing. Later when she got turned down again, and I left her at the door, she was headed toward the ........ Biscuit Co. on the trail of a rumor picked up in the lobby.

At 9:30, we were sent upstairs by the watchman and here the personnel manager interviewed us singly. The older women were turned aside with the assurance, "I am sure you wouldn't want this kind of work. We need strong, young girls to run back and forth." After they had left fifteen of us were hired for all kinds of work. We had to fill out application blanks, quite a job for the slower girls, and those that finished first were hired.

A team of five of us was put to work in the "Art Department" under a hard-boiled Irish forelady. I soon found she was hated by both porters and girls and reviling her was their chief pastime.

---

* This story of a candy worker's week is printed here because it presents in human terms the essence of facts contained in the report itself.

The girl in charge of our table was a thin little Italian with paper-white face and large eyes. She hated her job and was continually wishing she was married. She had been here two years, had started at $14 a week and had never been increased. The only promotion, she said, was to be put on piece work. A woman wrapper at a near-by table was working on piece. Her hands flew so fast one could scarcely see them. Her face was strained and tense, her eyes never left her boxes and paper. I asked how much she could average. "About $18 a week at this season," she replied without looking up. But she didn't do piece work all the time, the little Italian said. She was getting "too many shakes," in her wrapping.

The smallest girl on the new team, though not the youngest, was 19. She had been married a year but had left her husband and was now living at home. She would tell us long, sad tales of her married life.

About 11 o'clock I went to the dressing room to wash my hands. The place was fairly clean, although the odor was bad and on the walls were signs informing the girls that they must wash their hands after using the toilets. I looked about for soap and towels. The little liquid soap bowls were all empty and there were no towels in sight. "How do you wipe your hands?" I asked. "On toilet paper, or on your shimmy, if you like," answered one girl. The other girls in the place walked out without the formality of washing.

Our department was called the Ice Box. The temperature was a little above 50° and although most of the girls wore sweaters, they shivered at their work. The girls who tied and wrapped were permitted to sit on iron stools. But the cold from the floor crept up the metal and helped in the chilling process. Many of the girls had very bad colds. Two young Jewish girls who worked with us got disgusted at the cold and bored with the monotony of the work. We were tying a piece of tin-foiled candy to the leg of a chocolate turkey with a piece of yellow ribbon. After one of the forelady's harangues they decided to quit at once and went to tell her so. An argument followed in which the forelady's voice rose loud and shrill. "Go to hell, you old cat," shouted one of the girls and the two departed.

The three of us who were left at the table were much impressed by this show of independence. Jessie, the little Italian, told infamous stories about the forelady but when she appeared we all bent over our work and did not reply to her abuse.

At the 45-minute lunch period the girls retired to the cloak room on the same floor with the lunches they had brought from home. A stock room girl made coffee and sold it at three cents a cup. A few of us who had not brought lunch this first day slipped across the street to a lunch counter where we could get a bowl of soup or a sandwich for ten cents. The place was full of workmen and the air thick with frying grease but it was the only restaurant in the neighborhood. "Some of the factories have swell lunch rooms and serve you tea or coffee and sugar free," one youngster informed me. "But even at that, this is the best place I've worked in. Not so much overtime and they don't speed you so. I worked at ........ a year for $12 a week—a rotten dump, too. Here they start you at $14. I suppose they keep you there forever, too."

The next day was a holiday—election day—for which we would not be paid. On Wednesday, the turkey tying was resumed for the morning. Then in the afternoon, we did bulk packing, scooping up handfuls of hard candies from the trays into one pound boxes, closing them, weighing them on a little scale and then stacking them for wrapping. The hours dragged slowly. Between four and five the strain of standing became almost unbearable. We shifted from one foot to the other, trying to lean against the table occasionally for rest. By a quarter past five we were dull and speechless with fatigue. I turned to Jessie, "I'm all in. Do you get used to it so you don't mind it any more?" She replied. "I don't. Some of the girls don't seem to mind it, except when they're sick, but it sure gets me toward the end of the day."

On Thursday, I was sent to the next floor to work on a belt. It conveyed small pieces of hard candy from a cylinder to a table where it was spread out and cooled under three air-ducts. We pushed the candies back from the belt as they fell off and spread them over the table. After they dried we packed them in tin cans and stacked them away. The Italian woman with whom I worked said that almost every day a new girl was sent up to help her. "They don't stay. They quit. It's too hard for them."

I too, wanted to quit when the day was over. My palms were punctured full of holes from the sharp edges of the candy and my back ached from carrying the trays of tins and from bending over the too-low table.

On Friday I was glad to be put at a different job—fancy packing. Another small Italian girl—she looked a mere child—was my working partner. I asked her if she was just out of school and she replied that she had been married three years and had had a child that was born dead. She spoke with bitterness of her husband's attitude toward her work. He thought it "just play" and that she shouldn't be tired at night.

"My God! Tired! I just want to flop when I get home and instead I've got to get dinner."

We stood all day at this job, walking up and down the sides of the tables, each sticking a different kind of chocolate in each box. The girl in charge of this table was irritable all the time.

"What's the matter with May?" I asked my partner.

"Oh, don't mind her," was the reply. "You'd be mad too, if you had to look after all these new girls and didn't get any more than she does. She's been here five years and she's only making $15 a week. She hasn't any parents and has to keep herself on it."

"Why doesn't she leave and go some other place?"

"Yeh, and start in at $12 a week all over again. Each place you go to you get taken on as a new girl. The dippers are the only ones in this business that can make a living. Some of the speedy piece workers make good money at this time of the year, but they lose out in the summer when things are slack. I'd rather be on regular pay and this place ain't so bad. Say, you should see some of the factories I've worked in! This is a Paradise, you'd say."

On Saturday morning, the whole atmosphere of the place was different. The knowledge that 12:15 ended the day's work lightened all tension. When the bell rang, we rushed upstairs to the bookkeeper's window and lined up. Three day's pay is always held back but as I was leaving I got my full week. As the girls dressed to go home they grumbled about reductions for lateness, time lost, or mistakes they claimed were made in their rates. One girl said she never could figure out how she was paid but just took what she got and said nothing. I opened my envelope to see what had happened to me. I was disappointed. The enforced holiday of election day and the time lost on the morning of employment had in some way cut my prospective $14 a week to $10.40.

## METHOD OF INVESTIGATION.

The work of this investigation was done during the Spring and Autumn of 1927, so that part of the pre-Easter and all of the pre-Christmas peak seasons were covered. An attempt made to gather some material from up-state sources was unsuccessful due to the lateness of the season. The material presented here was obtained in Manhattan, Brooklyn and Long Island City. As New York City is the center of the candy-making industry of the state, if not of the nation, we believe that the conditions described are, with the exception of wage scales, representative of the state. Wages in up-state factories average, in 1927, over $2 a week less than in New York City, according to the figures of the New York State Bureau of Statistics and Information.

Three methods of securing material were used:

1—Interviews with factory managers or employers and official visits to the factory.

2—Inside investigation as workers in the factory.

3—Interviews with candy workers outside the factory wherever they could be reached.

During the Spring of 1927, letters were sent to the managers of twelve large representative firms, telling them of the work contemplated and asking for interviews and for permission to visit their plants. Six out of the twelve replied. Of these, five expressed their willingness to comply with both requests and were most courteous and co-operative. One granted an interview but refused to permit a view of the factory. At the end of the investigation, two more factories, in which the investigator had already worked, were officially visited with the permission of the management.

The investigator also interviewed the President of the National Confectioners' Association in relation to seasonal employment in the industry and the City Health Commissioner on the enforcement of sanitary regulations.

The bulk of the information presented herein in regard to actual working conditions was obtained from direct observation and work in the factory itself. Because of the difficulty in reaching the candy worker outside the factory, there was no other way in which the industry could be observed from the point of view of the worker. This opinion was endorsed by two progressive employers. When the investigator took a job in answer to an advertisement, neither the employer nor the girls with whom she worked knew who she was or what she was doing. The factory was not cleaned up for the occasion nor was the worker conscious of being "investigated."

The investigator and the assistants who helped her during the last six weeks of the study worked from one day to one week in each factory, depending upon the size and type of place and the opportunity for gathering information. While the choice of job had to be governed to some extent by chance, the fact that practically all candy factories enlarge their working forces from 20 to 50% during the rush season made it possible to cover a representative group.

Of the 25 factories in which jobs were obtained, 6 employed from 200 to 800 women; 11 employed from 50 to 200; 8 from 12 to 50. These figures are approximate.

One section of the candy-making industry could not be included—the very small, cheap kitchen factory, attached to a store or a small group of chain stores, employing two or three workers beside the owner and his family. They are usually housed in the basement or backroom of the store and display their fly-specked bulk candy in the store's window. These are probably the greatest sanitary offenders in the whole industry, but any unofficial investigation of them is impossible.

As might be expected of such low-paid workers, almost all of the candy workers live at home and have few organization contacts. Of the 85 girls interviewed in the course of the study, only six were reached through Y. W. C. A. industrial groups, four through a girl's home and three through personal introduction. All other interviews were obtained while working in the factory, during the lunch hour and while waiting with groups of applicants in outer offices to be interviewed for jobs.

## RECENT DEVELOPMENTS IN THE CANDY INDUSTRY.

During the last twelve years, the candy industry has undergone a tremendous development—a growth which has been frequently attributed to the Prohibition ·Amendment. According to the figures of the Department of Commerce, the American public, in 1925, consumed $248,883,257 worth of manufactured candy. In 1926, a report from 80% of the nation's candy makers indicate that that consumption had risen to $258,251,562 worth of candy—a $10,000,000 increase in a year. In an interview in the New York Times in November, 1927, a prominent candy manufacturer estimated that the industry would pass the half-billion mark in 1928.

With this growing prosperity has come increasing centralization of control, a quantity production at the top and on the other hand, a prolific crop of new, small, highly-specialized factories turning out expensive hand-made candies for the more epicurean taste.

In New York City, at least, the centralized control of the bigger factories has been accomplished through the investment of outside capital. Two large tobacco companies, with the profits gained from the public's increased cigarette consumption, have bought up at least five leading candy factories, all of which continue to operate under the old trade names. Two of these factories had previously been noted for the high standard of their product; they had been owned by families who had maintained an intimate interest in the business and a sense of responsibility regarding the output. Regarding any change in the quality of the product under the new "absentee ownership," this study has no information to offer. The consumer must depend upon his sense of taste for such enlightenment. But the experience of the investigators who worked in one of these plants both before and after its absorption, as well as interviews with workers in both of these places, would indicate that working conditions have deteriorated with corporation control and quantity production. In one factory, a decrease in the beginning wage, from $14 to $12 took place.

Nor is there any indication that this investment by large outside interests makes for better equipment in the factory itself. One of the largest of the companies so controlled has an obviously inadequate staff of porters and is still housed in an ancient building which no amount of effort could keep really clean.

The investigator was being shown through this plant by the obliging young manager. She noted the primitive, hit or miss seating arrangements—a kitchen chair there, a low stool surmounted by a box, here, and finally five really model seats. When she asked why these model seats were not in more general use, the young man replied: "We will probably get them in time but they are very expensive. We can't afford to put them in, all at once." This factory is owned by one of the richest of our national corporations.

At the opposite pole of the candy industry are the small, high-grade places mentioned before. Sometimes they are started by women who have taken "candy courses." A surprising number have succeeded in finding a market for their products at very good prices. In one case, the owner of such a place was a hotel owner who had formerly made candy for a few special customers in his hotel kitchen and had then found that the growing demand for fine quality candy justified the establishment of a separate factory. Maintaining the same high standard set in his own kitchen several years ago, he now employs seventy workers and maintains the most model candy factory found in the investigation.

Caught between this new quantity production of the big, advertising confectioner, catering to the popular taste through chain stores, cigar stands and department stores and the "class production" of a few quality manufacturers, the smaller factory owner, selling in bulk to the retailer, complains that he is being eliminated. Several manufacturers employing from fifty to a hundred girls, declared that they cannot compete with the new sales policies and advertising methods of those large firms which sell a standardized, low-priced product direct to the public. A representative of one of the biggest candy firms in New York City declared on the other hand, that the present speedy centralization in the industry was raising standards and making for greater stability of employment. There is no indication as yet that these claims are justified.

## THE CANDY FACTORY.

The twenty-five factories covered in the investigation represent four typical groups:

> 1—Large plants with well-known trade names selling their own brands of plain and fancy candies direct to the public through their own chain stores, cigar stores, drug stores, etc.
>
> 2—Large plants which manufacture nationally advertised brands of machine-made candies, such as chocolate bars, wafers, mints, etc., selling for five or ten cents; also wholesale supplies to jobbers and retailers. Employment in such places is less seasonal than in the first group.
>
> 3—The small high-class plants making expensive mixed candies. The work is almost exclusively hand-work and as a rule good working conditions prevail.
>
> 4—The small, cheap factory manufacturing bulk candy for the retail trade. This type is frequently dirty and unsanitary, its product unfit for consumption.

### Processes.

About sixty-one per cent. of all the workers in the candy industry are women. In 1923, there were 6,000 of them in New York City. They perform practically all of the operations except the actual making of the candy. Men do the cooking and men are also employed in the "hot rooms" where the gum candies are dried.

The *chocolate dipper* is the aristocrat of the candy trade. She is the best paid woman worker in the industry and her work requires a high degree of skill. During the peak season a dipper can average $35 and $40 a week. She sits at a table which holds containers of melted chocolate. With one hand she tosses the center or fondant into the chocolate, with the other she twirls it about in the soft mixture, then makes a deft distinguishing mark or circle on the top. One hand is constantly coated with chocolate. She sits all day in an atmosphere varying from 55 to 65 degrees.

The *bon-bon dipper* requires less manual skill. She dips the center in its creamed coating and twirls it about with a fork. Her hands are not coated and she can move about when she gets her supplies. The temperature in her section is normal.

*Machine dipping* or *enrobing* for hard-centered and for the less expensive grades of chocolates is becoming more common. If the machines are kept clean, it is also more sanitary. One group of girls feeds the candy centers onto the belt which carries them through the chocolate bath and through a cooling duct which sets the chocolate. On the other side of the machine, another group separates the candies which stick together and packs them in boxes. Where a "hand-dipped" appearance is desired on fancy chocolates, the candy on leaving the enrober passes on a belt between two rows of girls who mark the top of each piece with a chocolate stroke as it passes. These girls are the *strokers*. They sit all day, making the same monotonous gesture. The temperature in the enrobing room is always above normal, sometimes as high as 85 degrees. In smaller places where up-to-date ventilating systems have not been installed, the air is often stagnant and depressing.

*Packers* form the largest percentage of workers in the trade. One representative factory had 216 packers (general and belt packing); 50 dippers; 53 miscellaneous workers (peeling, decorating, nut shelling, etc.). The packer also ties and wraps at intervals. Her work is the most unskilled, the most irregular and poorly paid.

The simplest operation is bulk packing. In this the candy handled is all of one type. The investigator's first job consisted of scooping up in both hands, small candy Easter Eggs and pouring them into one pound boxes that were then stacked at the end of the table for wrapping.

*Fancy packing* may be of two kinds—spread packing at a long table or belt packing from a moving belt. These are the processes by which mixed candies are packed. In spread packing the worker moves along the table, takes each piece of candy from a tray in front of her and after sliding it into its paper cup, puts it in its proper place in the box. She packs after a certain pattern and in the more expensive candies, the strokes must be in the same direction, the candies uniform in size. Spread packing would seem to be the only process at which a sitting posture is not practicable, though even here, the outlay of sufficient capital to provide seats with rollers that would move along a groove in the floor, might solve this problem. Some of the larger factories have installed belt carriers in their packing departments. The belt with the empty boxes moves between two rows of girls. As it moves along, each girl contributes a piece of candy (sometimes 2 or 3 pieces) in its fluted cup, to its proper place in the box.

It was in belt packing that the investigator was initiated into the art of "sliding cups." The practice was commonly employed in all types of fancy packing.

> "You hold the pile of cups like this between your thumb and forefinger," explained the girl in charge. "They stick together as a rule, so you lick your middle finger like this, slide out the bottom one and put the candy in it."
>
> "Can't you have a sponge or something to wet your finger?"
>
> "It'd take too long. Just lick your finger and the cup will come off."

Theoretically, the wet finger of the worker touches only the bottom of the paper cup, but actually, as the box gets fuller, in order to squeeze one's candy into its proper place on the swiftly moving belt, one's moistened fingers come in contact with half the candy in the tray. The novice who attempts to keep her middle finger away from the candy soon finds that she can't keep up with the belt.

## Fatigue and the Belt.

In some factories, stools of sufficient height are provided so that the belt packer can sit at her work; in others, even the belt packer must stand. There is no practical reason why she should do so, unless the belt rotates so quickly that she must be on her toes to keep up with it.

During September, the investigator worked on the belt in one of the city's largest factories. The forelady pushed the button which started it going and the girls' fingers began to fly between the wooden trays and the moving boxes. The belt gained speed with each minute and with the increased speed the girls gradually arose from their seats to keep up with it. Occasionally the machinery would stop because the examiner at the end of the line would find too many mistakes, or because the boys were late in bringing up supplies. Each time the belt stopped, amid the imprecations of the forelady who was evidently being pushed from above for "production," the girls would slump back in their seats with sighs of relief and relaxation. Then the switch was pressed again and they bent forward. By four o'clock the newer girls began to complain that they ached all over. During the Christmas rush season, these packers worked until nine in the evening. The effect of these overtime hours will be discussed later in the report.

# GETTING A JOB.

"What kind of work are you looking for?"

"Any experience?"

"All right. We start at $12 a week. Write your name and address on here."

This was the typical interview preceding a job in a candy factory. Seven of the factories in which work was obtained had employment managers who required the filling out of a blank containing a few more questions and a slightly fuller verbal interview. In three factories of the smaller, cheaper type not even the name and address of the applicant were taken until she had worked two or three days and the payroll was being made out. In the meantime, she was addressed as "You there."

Jobs in candy factories are obtained either through advertisements or by "calling around" at the various factories during the rush season. Practically all of the bigger factories advertise for help during the pre-Easter and pre-Christmas seasons.

Fifteen out of the 25 jobs secured during the investigation were advertised in the newspapers. The other ten were secured by making the rounds. Waiting in the lobby to be interviewed, one picks up rumors of other opportunities.

> "Blanks aren't advertising any, but they're taking on a few girls. I'll go around there if I'm turned down here."
>
> "A friend of mine got in at ........ in Long Island City last week. It's not a bad place, but the trip isn't worth it. I'd rather make less in town."

## The Peak Seasons.

During September the average factory seems to take on almost anyone who applies, regardless of experience. The enormous turnover makes it necessary to have a few more girls on hand than are actually needed. But by November jobs are hard to find. The girls stop "shopping around" from one place to another. A hundred applicants may answer one ad for ten candy packers. The more experienced girls are taken, the others turned away.

Of the two peak seasons in the industry, the smaller one is the pre-Easter rush during February and March. After Easter and particularly after "Mother's Day," which has extended the employment season to some extent during the last few years, comes the big lay-off. The more experienced and skilled help is kept on, particularly the dippers. One factory guarantees its dippers $22 a week during the summer in order to hold them. Some of the other workers are put on part time; the rest are laid off.

By the first of September the big peak begins and lasts until Christmas. This is the period of greatest employment and of much overtime. Women who have been out of work all summer or who have worked in the country resorts drift into the candy factory. Regular candy workers, laid off the season before, come back for their old jobs.

In all but a few places, methods of hiring during this season are chaotic and unintelligent. The Sanitary Code requiring a medical examination on entry or else a "food handler's card" certifying that the applicant had been examined within a year, was enforced in only three of the twenty-five factories. (Medical inspection will be discussed in a later section.)

In two factories where the work consisted largely of spread packing, each girl was asked whether or not she felt able to stand on her feet all day as the work required. In the other 23 factories this question was not raised.

Working at a table with a team of new girls one hears the gossip of the various factories which the girls have "tried out" or heard about.

"Tomorrow, I'm going over to ......... I got a girl friend there and she says she can make $18 a week on piece. And you get a chance to sit down once in a while."

"Maybe they ain't taking on anyone and you'll lose out here."

"No danger. They need girls in this place and I'll say I was sick if I have to come back."

Another girl contributes. "You can make good money at Blank and Blanks, but I wouldn't work there. The forelady's a slave-driver and you work about 70 hours a week with overtime. They pay time and a half but it ain't worth it. Life's too short."

The investigator later found this estimate of Blank and Blank to be quite correct.

This shopping around for the best hours and wages while the rush is on, undoubtedly accounts for much of the tremendous turnover during the peak season. The employment manager of one large factory admitted a turnover of 300 and 400% during this season and a lay-off of 40% in the summer. As this factory pays a low beginning wage, this turnover figure is probably larger than for other plants of the same size.

As the season progresses and jobs, especially for the unskilled, become scarcer, the girls stick to what they have, while employment offices are still besieged by applicants. Superintendents and employment managers become more independent as the workers grow less so.

### Some Employment Methods.

In one large factory late in the season, an advertisement for 20 packers brought a crowd of more than a hundred women to the factory door by eight o'clock. They waited in the vestibule and on the outside stairs until nearly ten for the manager to appear. When he finally arrived, he ordered all the girls to the stairs. At intervals of about 20 minutes a new girl was called into the office. Between interviews he attended to other matters. At one-thirty in the afternoon, after six girls had been employed, he came out and announced to the still waiting crowd that "no more girls will be taken on today. Come back tomorrow." The bolder spirits among the tired applicants greeted the announcement with indignation and some profanity. One girl shook her fist in his face. The crowd disappeared gradually, grumbling and resentful of the wasted morning.

At another factory a crowd of 60 women waited in the dark hallway of a loft for the owner who had advertised for "candy packers." Stepping out of the elevator at nine o'clock he greeted the assemblage with surprised good-nature. "My Gawd! The Big Parade!" Then he continued. "I want just two very fast packers. Those that ain't fast and experienced can beat it."

"Why didn't you say so in your ad?" shouted one irate worker. All but six of the crowd melted away.

These methods were not typical of all the factories where the investigators applied for work. In at least half of them, the treatment of the girls, though hurried and perfunctory, was considerate and courteous, particularly where the hiring was done by a forelady or by a regular employment manager. In three places, the forelady in charge, needing no help herself, recommended places where she thought jobs might be secured. But in only three factories was there anything approximating a genuine interview or an attempt to fit the worker to the job best adapted to her. In all other cases, the hiring was done in the most casual manner. In a few months, many of those taken on would be fired in the same casual manner. Knowing this, these casual workers took little interest in their jobs and cared less about the maintenance of sanitary standards. Only in a few of the better-class places was there any "pride of work" among these young floaters, but on the other hand one found a general conviction that "candy's a rotten job, in which you never know what you're going to make or how long you'll be working."

## THE CANDY WORKER.

### Ages.

The candy trade is primarily an unskilled trade, employing young, inexperienced workers. While no recent figures on ages of the various groups of candy workers are available, at the time of the last census, three-fifths of the candy workers were under 21. It is unlikely that any great change has taken place since that time. Among the wrappers, tyers, strokers and packers particularly, the girl under 21 predominates. The hand dippers and bon-bon dippers belong as a rule to an older group, between 20 and 30.

Of the 85 candy workers of all kinds interviewed during the course of this study, 48 were between 16 and 20, inclusive; 25 between 21 and 30; 12 were over 30. The "over 30" group in a candy factory are most likely to be women between 40 and 50 or older. Women as old as 60 may be seen in some of the factories shelling nuts, pitting dates, and doing other odd jobs. The girl, too young to have acquired much skill or independence, the older woman left on her own resources without a trade and unable to do the heavy work of a charwoman, gravitate to the candy factory where all the skill required can be achieved within a few days. These older women do not as a rule work beside the young and more vigorous packers. Their's are the jobs in which speed is not an essential factor.

In one factory, however, in which the investigator worked as a packer, a little old lady of at least 65, worked a few feet away as a wrapper. She was tiny and frail, with fine, wizened features—so thin as to be almost transparent.

> "She could never hang on as a piece worker," confided a young Italian packer. "The girls all help her with her work and the boss is sorry for her I guess. If she loses this job, she'll never get another one."

## Nationalities.

The Italian and Italian-American girl predominated in all of the large factories, with a smaller group of Irish-Americans. During the last few years there has been an influx of Porto Rican workers (both men and women) into the industry. The Italian and other groups are apt to look upon these new Spanish-speaking workers with something of the same contempt and uneasiness with which the native Nordic worker looked upon the Italians a generation or two ago.

> "They work for almost nothing and do the decent workers out of jobs," complained one candy packer. "They live crowded together in one room and think that it's grand because it's better than they are used to, where they came from."

In some factories one finds a few Jewish girls and in a few, smaller better-class places, a sprinkling of German and Swiss girls. But the Italian is the backbone of the trade. Four out of the 25 factories covered hired a few colored girls. In one, where candied fruits and stuffed dates were packed, about half the workers were colored, the rest Porto Ricans and Italian.

## Background.

Seventy-four out of the 85 girls interviewed lived at home with parents or other relatives; six were married and lived with their husbands; only five "lived out"—four of these in a club where they paid $5 or $6 a week for room and board; the other, a more skilled worker, in a regular boarding house where she paid $10 a week for the same. This girl earned $15 a week in one of the better factories and claimed that she could not "make both ends meet" at this rate.

One out of the six employment managers officially interviewed by the investigator admitted that he would take only girls who lived with their families. As he naively put it, "No girl can live on $12 a week unless she lives at home. I won't take them on unless they say they live at home."

Other owners and managers interviewed expressed a preference for the "home girl" who could fall back on her family's support during the slack season, but declared that they would not refuse to hire a girl who lived away from home. Out of the 25 factories in which work was obtained, only five asked any questions about the worker's background. But there is a general conviction among the young candy workers that it is best to say one lives at home.

All but three of the girls living at home, with whom the investigators talked, contributed most or all of their earnings to the family income. A few gave regular amounts for their board and room—$7, $8 or $10 a week, and kept the rest for carfare and lunches. A majority handed over their pay envelopes intact to their mothers, who gave them back what was necessary for incidental expenses. During the slack season when so many workers are either laid off or put on part time, the family expense account is shaved down to meet the added burden of their support. It is obvious under these circumstances that the family really subsidizes the girl so that she can afford to work in a candy factory.

Three chocolate and bon-bon dippers were the sole support of their mothers. All of these three had been in the candy trade over eight years and were earning from $25 to $35 a week during the busy season.

It is the hope of getting into this better paid and more steadily employed group that keeps many of the candy workers in the trade. With the exception of a few girls who were studying stenography at night schools, and the large group that wanted to get married and stop working altogether, just as soon as possible, many of the girls explained that it was this chance of getting into "dipping" and making decent wages that kept them from deserting to such cleaner jobs as radio assembling, etc.

# WAGES IN THE CANDY INDUSTRY.
## Time and Piece Payments.

All but 5 of the 25 factories studied paid wages on both a time and piece basis, depending upon the operation and the experience of the worker. Four of the 5 factories which paid on a time basis exclusively manufactured a high-priced, quality product in which care in packing and handling were essential.

"Quality and the piece system won't go together," said the manager of one of these factories. "You can't place a premium on speed and expect a girl to do good work."

However, the one other factory which paid by the week was a small, dirty place on the East Side which manufactured peanut brittle and other nut candies. The reason for time payment in such a place could not be discovered.

A majority of the candy factories start their workers on a weekly wage, usually of $12, and then advance them to the piece system when they have gained sufficient speed to make this more profitable. The time payment period may last from two weeks to two months, but as a rule, the girl who cannot pack or wrap the minimum piece requirement at the end of a few weeks is let out. In many of the operations, however, such as stroking, belt packing and attending the enrobing machine, weekly or hourly rates are necessary. Or, a girl may work at spread packing one week on a piece basis and at the belt next week on a time basis.

In several factories, a "time and bonus" system of payment has been inaugurated. One of the largest and best of the New York City factories which for many years had paid on a time basis exclusively, has lately become converted to a method of this type, known as the Bedeaux System. Because it is likely that the system will gain further converts among candy manufacturers, the following statement of the candy worker's attitude toward it, is quoted from an investigator's report:

"Started work as a spread packer at $14.59 a week. There are no seats at spread packing. Hours are 8—5; 45 minutes for lunch. Tuesdays and Thursdays we work until six.

The Bedeaux Efficiency System is being introduced. Stop watches are used to get the girls' rate of speed. We are supposed to do a spread of 60 boxes in 2 hours, at a base rate of 31 cents an hour. For all boxes packed over that spread, we are paid a bonus of four different rates, increasing with the number of boxes packed. The limit is $20.80. The girls don't understand the system and resent it. They grumble that they are being cheated. The foreman says, 'If I explained it to you, you wouldn't understand it anyway, so there's no use wasting time." Information on earnings are posted each day after our names and the girls resent this too. On Monday, only seven out of the 34 girls in my department had earned additional rates, ranging from 5 cents to 80 cents.

Turnover is evidently increasing. Sixteen girls left this week. One girl said, 'The day I worked the hardest, I earned the least.'"

Another factory manufacturing five cent candy rolls employs a different type of bonus system. As an Italian worker describes the process:

"We pack 260 boxes a day for the boss. Then we get a bonus on the rest we pack. I've packed 400 boxes a day in the rush season, 120 pieces to a box. I can earn as much as $18 a week at this rate, but it don't last, of course. During the slack season when things are slow or when the machine breaks down and we have to wait around, I don't make more than $7.00 a week on part time. I've been in the trade seven years."

Another girl who has been in the same factory for over two years says that she averages $13 a week when she works "regular." But during the summer months, she averages $6.80 a week for three days' work.

## The Beginning Wage.

Thirteen out of the 25 factories studied paid a beginning wage of $12 a week; three paid $13 and $13.50 a week; nine paid $14 to $15, the latter rate being paid by only two firms.

Even this small beginning wage, however, is not always what it seems. In one factory where an investigator worked for $14 a week, her actual earnings amounted to $10.50 because of time lost through a holiday and for other reasons beyond her control. One morning the belt at which she worked broke down and the girls were sent home for the day. This breakdown or temporary stoppage of machinery and the consequent loss of time for which the girl is docked, is one of the worst wage abuses in the industry. In many factories in which workers are paid on a piece basis, they must clean the machine each day on their own time. In the smaller factories girls are frequently required to do such janitorial work as sweeping the floors and washing down tables on their own time. The ambitious piece worker frequently curtails her lunch period to make up for the time lost in this manner at the end of the day.

That the *beginning wage* in the candy industry is of greater importance than a similar wage would be in a more stable industry is due to the tremendous turnover of workers and the highly seasonal nature of the work. Each season, large numbers of girls are taken on anew for the more unskilled processes. These girls may have had candy experience in other factories, but as a rule they start at each new factory at the beginning wage.

After working in four factories, the investigator applied for work in the remaining plants as an experienced packer.

With the exception of one place in which she was put to work as an examiner at $15 a week, she started in at each new place at the beginning wage.

It is impossible to find the average time for which the packer is considered a beginner. The time differed with each factory and with the individual worker. In two of the best factories studied, the new girl was hired for two weeks at $12 a week. If she was found to be capable she was raised to $15 at the end of this time; if incapable of the quality and quantity of the work required, she was dismissed.

In another factory in which the beginning wage was $14 and where the manager had promised, "no girl stays at that wage more than a few months," the investigator found a number of girls who had been working over two years and were still making $14. That this was not due to their incompetence was evidenced by the fact that one of these girls was in charge of a table, and was considered a fast worker.

That this $12 and $14 "beginner's wage" may be an almost permanent wage for that large section of the candy workers which is laid off each season to begin anew the next in another factory is obvious from the number of girls encountered who had worked for more than a year and were still earning these amounts.

Forty-two of the 85 girls interviewed had worked in the trade from 6 months to 2 years and were still earning $14 or less.

Twenty-five had worked from 2 to 5 years and were earning less than $17.

*All but five were laid off or were put on part time during part of the year.* Eighty percent of the girls interviewed were packers, but the packers constitute the vast majority of the workers.

### Turnover.

No definite figure could be obtained as to the number of last season's workers who return each year to the same factory. Only a few plants keep adequate records from which such information could be secured. In those factories in which wages are higher and conditions good, interviews with managers and workers indicated that a large percentage of workers return each year to the same place.

In one factory with low wages and inferior standards, generally, 40% of the workers are laid off during the summer slack season, which has been reduced to two or three months, by refrigeration processes. Each fall a largely fresh supply of workers is taken on. Its constant advertisements for help during the five months preceding Christmas support the management's admission of a 300 to 400% turnover during this season.

### Earnings and Seasonal Employment.

Actual yearly earnings of women candy workers, particularly of the 33 to 45% who are laid off altogether during the slack season, could only be ascertained through extensive personal interviews of a large proportion of the workers. The figures on earnings issued by the Bureau of Statistics and Information are obtained primarily as a measure of trends of employment as measured in the number of workers employed and the total payroll reported for a week each month. The average is computed by dividing the weekly payrolls of the reporting factories by the number of employees actually on the payrolls at the time and as an index of changes in the earnings of wage workers month by month, it is useful. In an industry as seasonal as the candy industry, however, average earnings for a given week have little relation to the amount of money earned by the worker during the year and it is upon the yearly income that the worker must depend.

The chart shown on page 35 is based upon employment and payroll index figures of the Bureau of Statistics and Information from June, 1923, through December, 1927, and illustrates graphically the seasonal fluctuations. Reaching their

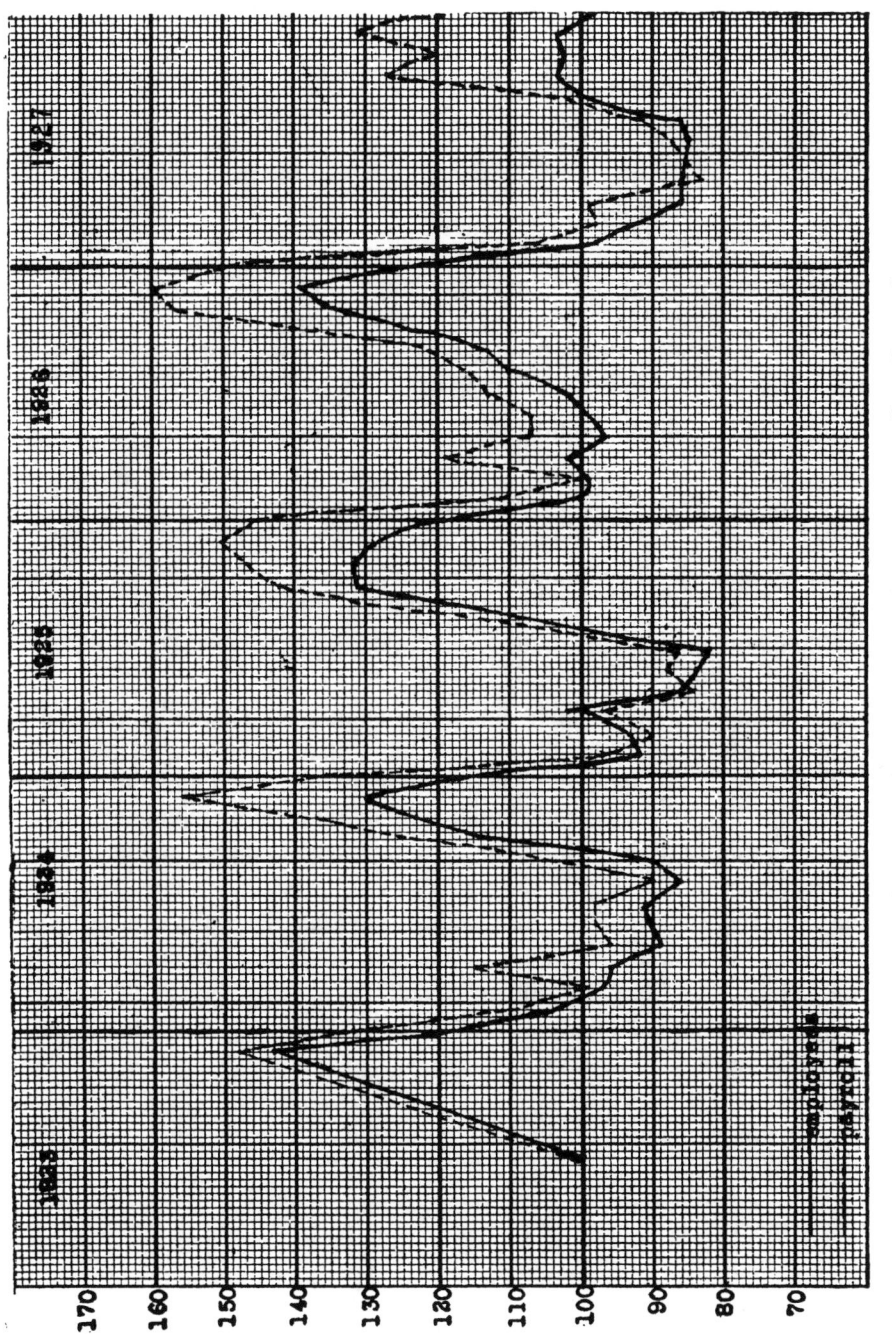

Employment and payroll chart for women candy workers in New York City
June 1923—December 1927.

peak in November of each year, at an index number of about 150, both employment and payrolls decline sharply through January and February; then rise slightly for the small spring peak of March to about 110; then decline to their lowest ebb of 84 or 85 during the late summer months.

In human terms these jagged curves are much more eloquent. A candy packer may be one of two hundred workers employed in a certain factory in March, a fairly normal month. By November she may be one of the force of 290 working during the pre-Christmas rush. After Christmas or after Easter she may be one of the 122 workers laid off for the summer until the fall rush season starts again. These 122 workers will "average" nothing at all during the summer slump unless they are able to find some other kind of employment.

Next to canning, the candy industry is the most seasonal in the state of New York. The large group of candy workers who must face the long seasonal slump each year as well as the many more put on part time employment must inevitably depress the living standards of the families on whose support they are thrown.

During 1924 and 1927, the chart shows that the Easter peak season brought no increase of employment, although the longer hours worked by the regular staffs made for a slight increase in average earnings. During 1927, both employment and payrolls, particularly the former, show a sharp decline. During the peak of 1927, as in 1924, the smaller number of employees in relation to the payroll indicates that average earnings for those employed were somewhat higher than in 1923, 1925 and 1926. This may, however, illustrate an isolated condition for the year rather than a trend of increase during the past five years.

**These figures should be taken as measuring fluctuations in employment.** They show how uncertain are the work and pay of the candy worker. But as a measure of individual earnings they are unsatisfactory. As the average is obtained by dividing the total payroll by the number on it, the higher wage of a small group, such as the dippers, at the top, pulls up the average above the earnings of the much larger group at the bottom.

### Median Earnings.

What *we* want to know is this—how many girls are in the low-wage groups? The best answer to this question is the *median,* that is, the wage at which the group divides, half earning less and half earning more. This median is always lower than the average. For this reason, we find more significant for our inquiry the study made by the Bureau of Women in Industry on this subject.

This is the last detailed report on earnings of women workers in the candy industry, in which earnings are considered in relation to hours of work, and was published by the New York State Department of Labor (Bulletin 121) in 1923. This report was based on the study of payrolls for a week during March, the height of the small pre-Easter peak season. The following were the *median* earnings of women workers during this week—that is, 50% of the workers in each classification earned *less* than these specified wages:

Median wage for
- All workers .................. $13.75
- Full time .................... 15.00
- Overtime .................... 16.65
- Undertime ................... 11.75

(45% of the workers worked undertime in N. Y. C.)

One woman candy worker out of every two earned less than $13.75.

One-third earned less than $12.

Sixteen dollars or more was earned by less than one-third.

Twenty dollars or more was earned by 14%. Only 4% earned more than $25.

As was said before, it is impossible to calculate yearly earnings of the large number of workers laid off altogether during the slack season or to know to what extent these workers obtain other employment. The few interviews obtained indicate that many of the young girls stay home and pick up odd jobs during the summer, depending largely upon their families to carry them over. Some of the older girls take jobs in near-by country resorts. One employment manager thought that many of his casual workers found places in two large biscuit factories during the summer. The fact that other large absorbers of unskilled female labor, such as radio assembling, box-making, etc., have their slack and peak seasons at similar times must make the summer employment of the part-time candy worker a precarious matter.

The forty-five percent of the candy workers who even in March worked less than their scheduled hours and whose *median income* was $11.75, were receiving less than the lowest possible estimate of a fair wage, even for the girl who lives with her family. The National Industrial Conference Board, a research organization supported by a group of large employers, in its "Cost of Living in New York City in 1926," estimates a fair minimum of $12.80 a week for the industrial girl who lives at home. These figures are far below those of more impartial and official sources. Bringing the report of the Factory Investigation Commission of 1913 up to date by increasing it according to the index figures of the increase in the cost of living since that time, we find that the *subsistence minimum* of the girl living alone in New York City in 1926 was $16.07. A subsistence minimum cannot be called a fair wage.

That the girl who lives at home, or in a subsidized club house and who earns less than her actual maintenance cost as an individual, is partially supported by her family or by society; that the factory paying less than a fair wage is subsidized by that family or by society, is an unmistakable conclusion.

## Budgets.

An attempt to obtain cost of living budgets from girls who lived at home was unsuccessful. For the most part these girls turn over their pay envelopes to their mothers and have no idea how the money is spent. The following two budgets secured from candy workers who live away from home may give some indication of how the low-wage worker without a family to fall back on manages to exist.

The first budget was made out by a girl of 18 living in a girl's club. She earned $14 a week.

| | |
|---|---:|
| Board and Lodging (with 2 meals) | $6.00 |
| Extra Lunches at 25c | 1.50 |
| Clothing | 2.80 |
| Doctor and Dentist | .50 |
| Carfare | .70 |
| Recreation | .50 |
| Self-improvement (Reading Matter, etc.) | .30 |
| Church | .10 |
| Savings | — |
| Cleaning and Laundry | .30 |
| Incidentals | 1.00 |
| | $13.70 |

The second girl reporting earned $15 a week and lived in a boarding house.

| | |
|---|---:|
| Board and Lodging (with 2 Meals) | $10.00 |
| Extra Lunches | 1.00 |
| Clothing | 2.00 |

| | |
|---|---|
| Doctor and Dentist | — |
| Carfare | .80 |
| Recreation | .40 |
| Self-improvement | .20 |
| Church | — |
| Savings | — |
| Cleaning and Laundry | .30 |
| Incidentals | .50 |
| | $15.20 |

When it was pointed out to this girl that this total was more than she earned she replied:

> "I know it. I don't know how I manage. Some weeks I go over $15 and some weeks I squeeze under. I've had to borrow money several times and I need my teeth fixed but I can't afford to go to the dentist. I've got to get some other kind of work or move into some place where I can get cheaper board."

The first girl, an intelligent little packer, was questioned concerning the comparatively large clothes item of $145.60 a year. She replied:

> "I know it looks big, but that's because when you earn only $14 a week you never have enough money on hand to buy good things that will last. I try to get fairly good shoes, paying about $5 or $6 for them when I have the money, but once I needed shoes and couldn't spare that much so I bought a pair of $1.49. They were paper, of course, even the tops, and they didn't last a month. Lots of girls I know buy paper shoes all the time. They can't afford any others. The trouble is, we've got to buy clothes when we need them and whenever we happen to have the money on hand. You're

bound to get cheap stuff that way and so you pay more for clothes in the long run than people who have more money."

## HOURS IN THE CANDY INDUSTRY.

Twenty-one out of the 25 factories studied had a scheduled work-week of 49 hours. That scheduled working hours in a candy factory have very little relation to hours actually worked may be seen from the following figures from the study made by the State Bureau of Women in Industry (Dept. of Labor, Bulletin 121).

During the pre-Easter week in March in which the study was made in New York City,

47% of the candy workers worked full time
45% worked undertime
6% worked overtime
2% unspecified hours.

A higher percentage of overtime would be found during the fall; a far larger percentage of undertime would be found in summer.

The scheduled work-day in a majority of the factories is from 8 A. M. to 5:30 P. M. and from 8 to 1 on Saturday. Sixteen of the factories studied had 45 minute lunch periods; six, half hour lunch periods and three gave an hour for lunch.

The longest scheduled hours were found in two of the largest factories, 8 to 5:45, with half an hour for lunch.

The shortest hours were found in two smaller factories of the better class—8 to 5 with full hour for lunch. All but one factory gave a Saturday half-holiday.

As was said above, these scheduled hours mean very little for a large number of workers. Some undertime is almost universal during the summer. Overtime is almost universal in the months preceding Christmas. This is particularly true of those factories which sell fancy candies direct to the public through their own chain stores. The large wholesaler who sells through jobbers is better able to spread his work over the season. Many of the small manufacturers selling in bulk to the retailers are also less affected by the Christmas rush. People who buy candy for Christmas presents usually purchase advertised brands of boxed chocolates.

### Overtime.

Overtime in the type of factory supplying such candies may run from four or five hours a week (within the limit set by the 54-hour law previous to 1928) to as much as seventy hours, in violation of all law, including that of Sunday rest.* Six of the 25 factories were guilty of some violation of the hours law during the period in which the investigators worked in them. Of the other 18, it can only be said that they may or may not have violated it at some time. A few probably did not. But it remained for one of the largest and best known plants, controlled by large corporation interests, to work its employees up to 65 and 70 hours a week. A part of the investigator's report on this factory may be quoted:

> "The employment manager told me that they were working overtime, but he did not tell me that overtime hours were from six to nine every night except Thursdays and Saturdays (with half hour dinner period after 5:30), Saturday afternoons, and on Sundays from 9 to 4 P. M.
>
> My first impression of ———— was of Mrs. B, the forelady, stalking down the room and announcing that everyone should come to work the following Sunday. The girls didn't want to work but said they had to.
>
> The first evening I worked till nine, I had a chance to talk with the girl next me. 'I've got a headache,' she said. 'And I've got a backache,' added the girl across the way. I asked Sadie if we had to work such long hours and she replied: 'They can't make you, but

---

* The modified 48-hour law which went into effect Jan. 1, 1928, permits a total of 72 hours of overtime, distributed through the year.

they make it mean for you if you don't. This year, we've been working nights and Saturday afternoons since August.'

'But it's against the law,' I protested. 'Yeah, but they get 'round it. Once in a while, if you have a very good excuse, they let you off.'

She had been working here for seven years and said the same thing happened almost every year.

All the girls seemed tired out in the mornings. I asked a girl how she felt as we started work. 'Dead, as usual,' she replied.

Time and a half was paid for overtime and most of the girls were making from $19 to $22 a week packing. Yet a majority of them were complaining about the overtime constantly."  *

This factory was unusual in that it paid time and a half for overtime hours. In almost all the others a straight hourly or piece rate was paid. Four gave a dollar for the three hours from 6 to 9. One gave the girls 75c for dinner in addition to this one dollar.

Several factories have attempted to meet the rush problem by hiring a separate group of women for work from 6 to 9 or 10 in the evening, appealing especially to those married women who can leave their children with their husbands during the evening and who may want to earn extra money at this season. Three factories paid such extra help $1 for the evening's work.

### Overtime and Fatigue.

While it is undoubtedly true that the overtime work of the peak seasons is welcomed by those poorly paid workers

---

* A report of illegal overtime hours at this factory was made to the Factory Inspection Division which investigated and verified the violation, turning the case over to the Attorney General's office for prosecution. When the case came up for a hearing in February, the employers pleaded guilty to working one girl in excess of the legal limitation and were fined $20 for a first offense.

who lose so much time during the summer months, there was abundant evidence that the long hours impose a serious strain on all but the most vigorous girls. Even with the normal working day of nine hours without overtime, the girls who stand on their feet all day and the strokers whose work consists of one monotonous gesture of the hand, begin to "slump" and to complain of fatigue toward the end of the day.

During the investigator's first week in the factory, she was inclined to believe that the almost unendurable fatigue of the last hour was due to the newness of the experience. But as the season progressed this last hour continued to be a nightmare. A few of the more vigorous girls did not seem to mind it. "You get used to it after a while," said a big German girl who had worked as a spread packer for three years. "The first few months, I thought I'd pass out about 4 o'clock, but I don't mind it now except when I'm not feeling well."

However, nine out of ten of the girls interviewed complained of fatigue either from standing or from speed and monotony. Toward the end of the day, this fatigue was noticeable to the most casual observer, either in the general lassitude and "letting down" or the restlessness and irritability of the workers.

A short rest period during the middle of the morning and a slightly longer one in the afternoon would do much to make the workday happier and would undoubtedly increase production during the last hour or two of the day.

## THE HEALTH OF THE CANDY WORKER.

The candy industry is not a hazardous one and serious accidents are rare. Neither is there any distinctive occupational disease except, perhaps, the "chocolate dermatitis" of the chocolate dipper. The dipper's hand is constantly covered with chocolate coating which frequently results in an irritation and rash on the skin. When such a condition occurs, the dipper is usually put on other work until it clears up. In packing hard, sugared candies the hands are frequently cut and irritated by the sharp edges of the candy and furuncle of the finger is fairly common among packers of this type.

In a recent study of hygiene in the candy industry, the State Bureau of Women in Industry found that only one factory out of the thirty studied kept complete dispensary records. A report based on the records of this one large plant has been published by the State Department of Labor in a leaflet called "Analysis of the Medical Records of a Candy Factory."

The medical investigator for the Bureau found that among the 310 women workers listed, there were 286 cases of minor injuries recorded during the year. The most common medical conditions reported were headache ("one of the commonest symptoms of fatigue"), dysmenorrhea, and upper respiratory infections. A much higher percentage of upper respiratory infections in the chocolate packing and particularly in the chocolate dipping departments, than in other departments, indicates the danger of the "cool room" temperatures to less robust workers. A higher percentage of dysmenorrhea was also found in these departments.

Any detailed study of this subject was outside the scope of the present investigation. However, the actual experience of the investigators as well as interviews with 85 workers brought out the two most common causes of complaint among the candy workers—fatigue and chill.

Of the 85 girls interviewed, only six said they did not mind standing on their feet all day. The rest all declared that they "knew it wasn't good for them." The strokers who usually sit at their work, making marks on the wet chocolates, declared that the monotony and eye-strain made them "woozy" and that their right arms ached at the end of the day. Many of the belt packers complained that the speed of the belt and the strain of keeping up with it kept them tense and tired all the time. In many factories, the belt packer also stands at her work and so has the double strain.

### The Seating Problem.

In only three out of the 25 factories studied were seats provided for all operations. In two, only dippers and nut sorters were seated. In 20, seats were provided for some operations—wrapping, tying, stroking and some belt packing—but a majority of the workers had to stand. In one factory the stools provided were much too high and the girls stooped uncomfortably at their work.

In one large "daylight" plant in Long Island City, good stools with backs were provided for all workers. But when the investigator after two hours of standing, mistakenly sat down on the stool behind her, the forelady hurried up and informed her that "no sitting was allowed at packing—only at wrapping and tying." The stools, however, were a boon to the tired workers toward the end of the day. They could "sneak a sit" every little while when the forelady wasn't looking. The management probably counted on their doing this, as nothing was ever done about it.

Forty-eight out of the 85 girls interviewed were under 21. Many of them were 16 and 17. That girls of this age should not be required to spend nine hours a day on their feet should be obvious to anyone. That the only operation in a candy factory at which sitting is impractical is that of spread packing is the opinion of all investigators of the industry and the admission of many factory owners. As has been said before, even here the outlay of sufficient capital to provide the type of sliding seats used in some other kinds of assembling work could solve this problem. In the meantime, a few seats in this department, on which the girls could take turns at resting for a few moments occasionally, is not an unreasonable demand. In all other candy operations, continuous standing is inexcusable on any ground other than that of a greed which would speed the worker to the limit of her endurance.

The Labor Law of the State of New York, Section 146, reads as follows on this subject: "A sufficient number of suitable seats, with backs, where practical, shall be provided and maintained in every factory and mercantile establishment * * * for female employees, who shall be allowed to use the seats to such an extent as may be reasonable for the preservation of their health. In factories, female employees shall be permitted to use the seats whenever the work in which they are engaged can be properly performed in a sitting posture."

The wording of the law leaves much to the interpretation of the Industrial Commissioner, but "a sufficient number of suitable seats" where the work permits of sitting, can mean nothing less than a seat for each individual worker.

### Chill.

The second most common cause of discomfort, if not of ill-health among candy workers is the cold in the chocolate dipping and packing rooms. In spite of the fact that almost all girls in these departments wear sweaters—frequently dirty sweaters worn over the white aprons decreed by the management—there is constant grumbling in many factories because of the chilliness of the rooms. Chocolate dipping and packing can evidently be done in an atmosphere of 65° F, since this is the temperature maintained in several of the best plants. But in spite of this, in two plants where investigators worked, wall thermometers registered as low as 45° at times. The new girls suffered particularly from the cold. When they complained the forelady said, "We can't help it. The chocolate won't dry if we make it any warmer." By five o'clock some of the girls were fairly blue from cold.

While 45° was not a typical temperature, in twelve of the factories studied thermometers rarely registered above sixty. Many of the girls in these departments seemed to have permanent colds.

No generalizations are possible concerning the general health standards of such a group as the candy workers, but the personal observation of the investigator led her to believe that the majority of the women employed in candy factories could scarcely be called sturdy. Many bore unmistakable signs of malnutrition and the lack of care that comes with poverty-stricken backgrounds. The husky immigrant girl of sturdy peasant stock is notable for her absence. The undersized, white-faced girl, who at 20, looks 15, was much more common. It would seem that the stronger, more independent girl soon forsakes candy for some more lucrative field of employment. The apparent health of the worker differed somewhat with the factory. In two plants where something approximating a genuine medical examination took place on entry, a higher physical standard was obvious.

### Medical Examination.

The New York State Law (Sanitary Code, Rule 346) requires that in cities of the second and third class the proprietor of every candy factory shall have in his possession for each employee, a medical certificate "of not more than six months' standing" which certifies that the employee is free from "such contagious, communicable or skin diseases as the Public Health Council may deem necessary for the safeguarding of the public health." In addition to this, the Labor Law provides for a physical examination of any employee whenever a medical inspector of the department of labor shall demand it.

New York City, being a city of the first class, is not affected by this provision of the sanitary code, but the Department of Health has adopted this code for New York City, except that a yearly, rather than a bi-yearly health certification is required. Every "food handler" in New York City is supposed to have filed with his employer a "food-handler's card" issued by the Board of Health, signed by a Board inspector, by the company's or his own private physician and stating that he or she has been examined and found free of communicable diseases.

It is obvious that a genuine enforcement of such a provision is a task that no busy and inadequately equipped department of health is equal to. That the law is an entering wedge for some competent system of inspection in the future, that it at least calls the attention of worker and employer to the necessity of some standard of hygiene, that in the case of those workers actually examined, incipient conditions may be discovered and corrected as a result of discovery, is about all that can be said for it at this time.

In only two out of the 25 factories covered did regular part-time physicians examine the worker before she started working. In one other, the applicant was requested to get her food-handler's card from the Board of Health before she could be taken on. These examinations were perfunctory, consisting of a few taps on the chest, a look at the throat and a few questions as to whether or not she had had typhoid or tuberculosis. In 12 other places, investigators were taken on without a single question concerning their health, but questioning of older girls revealed the fact that visiting physicians did come around in due time to look over the girls. If one were hired the week following this visit, one might go on for months without an examination. In only one of these twelve factories did the examination take place while the investigators were working. In the other ten factories covered none of the girls questioned had ever heard of health examinations.

### Enforcement of Health Regulations.

Real enforcement of the health examination provision by the Board of Health would undoubtedly require an inspector on the doorstep of every factory all during the peak season, due to the tremendous turnover of workers. As this is obviously impossible, it would seem that only the education of the candy worker and of the factory owner himself and the complete cooperation between factory owners and the health department can really safeguard the candy-eating public from whatever risk is involved in eating food handled by dirty or diseased workers. If every factory owner were to require a "health card," not more than six months old, from each applicant for work (a card which the worker could take with her when she left the factory); if in addition to this the employer would provide for frequent and regular examinations of his staff by a visiting physician or a board of health inspector, much of this risk would be obviated and the preventive value to the worker would be enormous.

Well-equipped dispensaries, in charge of trained nurses in the larger plants could do much to raise the health standards of the factory. Plants too small to provide such facilities could arrange for such "travelling nurse" service as is provided by the Henry Street Settlement. Four out of the 25 plants studied had excellent dispensaries with trained nurses in charge; five more had some sort of dispensary in charge of "practical nurses." These nine also had visiting doctors.

# FACTORY SANITATION AND THE CONSUMER.

## Plant Cleanliness.

Aside from the almost complete disregard of the health examination codes in the candy industry, the sanitary standards of the factory itself are of intimate concern to the candy consumer. While it is probably unreasonable to expect the same standard of cleanliness and order in an industrial plant employing a hundred or more workers as one would expect in a first-class individual kitchen, the fact that a few plants do approximate this high standard shows the possibility of maintaining clean factories.

Two of the plants studied could be called "model" factories from a sanitary viewpoint. In the smaller of these, employing about seventy women, not only was the factory spotless and odorless and the workers clean and healthy looking, but the products used in the manufacture of the candy were quite obviously of the best possible quality.

Among the larger plants, five were as clean as one could reasonably expect from organizations employing several hundred people. But in three out of these five, the general cleanliness of the plant itself was somewhat offset by the practices of the workers and the lack of enforcement of sanitary regulations. The rule that workers should wash their hands after leaving the toilets was not enforced; candy dropped on the floor was picked up and put back in the box (an almost universal practice); while washing facilities were adequate, towels were usually missing, or the practice of sliding cups by licking the finger, was indulged in.

Sanitary conditions in some of the smaller plants manufacturing cheap candies were appalling. Floors and stairs were coated with sugar and fallen candy; machinery and work tables were apparently never scrubbed; the odor of rancid chocolate permeated the atmosphere; and worst of all was the odor of the dressing rooms. In one factory in which the work rooms were fairly clean and in which the girls were expected to wear clean, white aprons, the one dressing room containing three toilets and two washbowls was so malodorous as to be sickening. In this factory, the brush used to remove finger prints from the boxed chocolates frequently fell on the floor, was picked up again and used. On one occasion, some old chocolates were taken out of stock to fill a rush order. Tiny worms on the top of the chocolates were industriously brushed off with this same brush.

In all but a few small places, the workers are required to wear caps and aprons. Sometimes these caps and aprons are bought outright from the factory and laundered by the worker. Frequently the worker buys them outside. In a few factories the worker is provided with an apron by the management and is then charged 10 or 15 cents a week permanently for its laundering. The sanitary value of this protective covering is frequently annulled by the sweaters which so many workers wear over their aprons. The dirty sweater sleeve is the garment which most frequently comes in contact with the candy.

## Washing Facilities.

The matter of proper washing facilities is of great importance in the candy industry in which the hands of the workers come into such intimate contact with the product. In such processes as chocolate dipping and date "rolling" particularly, the cleanliness of the worker's hands is of primary importance.

Most of the factories covered met the letter of the law in providing sinks and wash bowls with hot water. But in many cases the washing facilities were too far from the toilets to serve the purpose for which they were most needed. In many, the hot water was boiling water, used to sterilize vessels, etc., so that the worker couldn't use it unless individual bowls were also provided; soap was frequently missing. The law prohibits the use of a common towel but does not demand individual towels and so in a majority of the factories covered there were no towels in evidence or the supply of paper towels was exhausted about half the time.

Whatever the background of the average candy worker, it is safe to assume that if cleanliness were made easy and attractive to her, she would follow the line of least resistance and obey the sanitary regulations. Her hands get sticky and dirty from the sugared product and she would be more comfortable with them clean. While it is exceedingly difficult for any factory manager or forelady to enforce the washing rule, (too many of them seem never to have heard of it), a clean, light wash-room kept in proper order, with plenty of paper towels, soap and hot water continuously on hand would undoubtedly encourage cleanliness and raise the hygienic level of the factory generally. A monitor for each table could also keep the girls reminded of the washing rule. As it is, in many plants, cleanliness is made as inconvenient as possible.

### Difficulties of Classification.

It is difficult to draw up any hard and fast classification of "good," "bad" or "fair" for the 25 factories covered in this report, except in the cases of those few which were either excellent or impossible in all respects. One big "model" plant which prides itself on its high standards had no towels in its dressing rooms while the investigators worked there and paid no attention to the personal cleanliness of the employees. On the other hand, the one large factory which made some attempt to enforce the washing rule by keeping a woman in the dressing room to remind the girls and to clean the bowls (she spent most of her day with her nose buried in a dime novel), permitted finger licking and violated the 54-hour law.

Speaking generally, as regards sanitation, about half of the 25 factories covered seemed passably clean. This is given only as an individual judgment and standards of cleanliness differ widely among individuals. Sanitary standards in the candy industry are probably no worse and may be better than in many food-producing industries. The handling and preparation of food on a large scale is rarely a spectacle to delight the fastidious. However, the production of candy in almost all of the small, cheap places and in a few of the bigger and better known ones, is unnecessarily dirty. (This is the type of candy most frequently bought by school children in small stores and stands.) With the exception of a few well-known brands of wrapped bars, chocolate wafers, etc., produced under exceptionally fine conditions, one may safely say that cheap candy is too "cheap" in all respects to be fit to eat.

### Some Odious Comparisons.

It would be unfair to compare conditions, hours and wages in a plant selling fine candies at two dollars a pound with those in a "mass production" factory selling mixed candies at fifty cents a pound. In making the following comparisons, we have chosen factories similar in output and size in order to show that decent standards of hours, wages and cleanliness may be maintained at a profit because it is actually being done:

**A** is a factory employing about 350 women. It is not an ideal plant but it is light, airy and comparatively clean. The beginning wage is $14.40 a week, the scheduled work week 49 hours. There is a medical examination on entry and a high standard of personal cleanliness is demanded of the girls. Overtime in the rush season seems to be kept within the legal limitation. Finger licking at spread packing is forbidden. Seats are provided in all operations except spread packing. A cheerful lunch room in which tea, coffee, sugar and milk are given free, is provided. A half-time doctor and a trained nurse are in attendance.

**B** is a factory of similar size and selling its product at a similar price. Its building is old and dreary, obviously converted from other uses. The management has too small a staff of porters with which to keep it clean. The workers are lax in their personal standards and the dressing rooms and washing facilities are no encouragement to improvement. The beginning wage is $12 a week. During the rush season, overtime frequently exceeds the legal limitation. There is constant grumbling among workers and a tremendous turnover of workers during the busy season. Factory conditions are generally chaotic. Medical examinations are held some time during the year and a rather poor dispensary is presided over by a practical nurse.

The following two factories are picked for comparison because they are somewhat similar in size and both specialize in the packing of plain and stuffed dates and in candied peels:

**M** is housed in a modern building in Brooklyn and kept freshly painted and very clean inside. From May to September a 44-hour week prevails and one week's vacation with pay is given. Hours are from 8 to 5. The minimum wage is $16 after six weeks' trial at 32 cents an hour. Fifty percent. of the workers make over $1,000 a year. The girls are carefully watched by a trained nurse and an assistant nurse to see that they do not work so fast as to tax their strength. Seats are provided for all operations. Since the introduction of the five-day week and the practical ironing out of peak seasons by refrigeration, turnover has been cut in half, overtime is almost unknown and when necessary occurs on Saturday afternoons. There is an excellent dispensary with two nurses, a visiting doctor and regular medical examinations twice a year. Follow-up work into the homes of sick workers is done by the head nurse.

There is also an intelligent and sympathetic woman personnel manager. The plant had a cheerful lunchroom with facilities for warming food, a separate recreation room with phonograph and records. A general spirit of cheerfulness and good feeling prevails. Dividends do not seem to have suffered.

**N** manufactures and packs the same type of product selling at about the same price. It occupies five floors of a modern building near the river front, but the inside of the building is dirty and littered with crates and boxes and is sickening with the combined odor of human bodies and date mash. The stairs and floors are caked with sugar. The packers start at $12 a week, the "date rollers" on piece averaged $13 and $14. Many of the girls who did this latter work which consists of taking the pitted date between the two palms of the hands and rolling it into shape and smoothness, then making an indentation with the thumb nail into which a piece of walnut was inserted, were unspeakably dirty—the most completely submerged looking workers the investigator had ever seen. Hours were long with much overtime. A little Italian forelady, apparently about 20, did the hiring and firing. No medical examination had been heard of by anyone in the room. Dressing rooms very inadequate and dirty. Practically all workers were seated, but on kitchen chairs too low for the tables. There was no lunch room.

## SUMMARY.

The facts disclosed in the present study, supplemented by the figures furnished by the State Department of Labor would indicate that the two major tragedies of the industrial worker's life—low wages and unemployment—are particularly keen in the case of the candy worker. Perhaps no other group of women workers in our midst is so unorganized, so young and so inarticulate—therefore so helpless.

### Wages.

Working conditions and wages for women candy workers seem to have altered little since the extensive study of 1923 revealed the fact that half of the candy workers in New York City were earning less than $13.75 a week, during the comparatively busy month of March; that the 45% who worked undertime at this season were earning less than $11.75. The example of the candy packer interviewed in 1927, who earned $18 a week during the rush season and $7 a week during the slack season is typical of wage conditions in many factories. These wages average less than the most conservative conception of a fair wage.

### Hours.

In spite of the reasonable scheduled work week of 49 hours which prevailed in a majority of the 25 plants studied, extreme undertime, down to two or three days' work a week (for those workers kept on the payrolls during the slack season) is common during the late winter and all of the midsummer months.

During the rush season from September to Christmas, overtime hours extend the work week from 54 in many to 65 and 70 hours in some plants.

During the *average* month of March, only 47% of the candy workers worked their scheduled hours.

## Unemployment.

In addition to the large number of workers who are put on part-time after Christmas and during the summer months, about 33% or more of the candy workers are laid off altogether during these dull seasons. It is impossible to ascertain how many of these floating workers are able to obtain other employment at such times, but the fact that the labor market is flooded with all types of unskilled workers released from other seasonal industries at the same time, makes it probable that large numbers of candy workers must depend upon their relatives to "keep them going" over this season.

## Hygiene and Sanitation.

The almost complete disregard for the sanitary code requiring a medical examination before employment, or its purely nominal enforcement by means of a perfunctory yearly examination violate either the letter or the spirit of a code drawn up to protect the consuming public from dirt and infection. In only three of the 25 factories covered was an examination or a food-handlers' card required on entry. In 12 others, a yearly examination took place sometime and in the remaining ten, the workers had never heard of examinations.

Aside from this inadequate enforcement or disregard of the health examination, the most common hygienic abuses were the failure of the girls to wash their hands after using the toilets (due largely to inadequate or inconvenient washing facilities); wetting the fingers with sputum when packing with paper cups; using candy dropped on the floor.

Three factories were very clean; ten more were passably clean; twelve were unnecessarily dirty.

The personal cleanliness of the worker's appearance usually paralleled the state of the factory.

Fatigue, due largely to long hours of standing on their feet; and chill, due to unnecessarily low temperatures in the chocolate dipping and packing departments seem to be the chief causes of complaint and ill-health among the candy workers.

Conditions described in the candy industry are probably more or less typical of those in all low-wage, seasonal industries in which the workers are young and unskilled. Evidently fair wages and fair conditions cannot be left to the altruism of the individual employer where the worker is unable to enforce her own demands. In some cases, fair wages and conditions are granted voluntarily by far-sighted and intelligent owners who realize that such conditions make for greater efficiency and bigger profits in the long run. But on the whole, the young unorganized worker must look to the public for some protection until she is able to protect herself.

The possibility of trade union organization among the candy workers is remote. Some attempt at organization was made a few years ago but failed, due largely to the youth and fluctuating nature of the group.

## RECOMMENDATIONS.

On the basis of the facts discovered in the present study and in others previously made, the Consumers' League of New York, makes the following recommendations on wages, hours, hygiene and sanitation in the candy industry.

1—That the Department of Labor, through the Industrial Commissioner, be empowered to name a committee of employers, employees and an impartial chairman to discuss wage conditions in a given industry, which in the opinion of the Commissioner, based on previous investigation by the Labor Department, pays less than a fair wage. While the committee would have no mandatory power to fix and enforce wage rates, such conferences between employers and employees under the direction of the Labor Department, with full publicity given to all proceedings and decisions, would do much to let in light on our industrial dark spots; to educate employers to the necessity of better management methods (that have already made possible fair conditions in individual plants); and would undoubtedly be an effective aid to the unorganized worker.

2—Strict enforcement of the new modified 48-hour law, with particular reference to its overtime provisions. This enforcement is particularly necessary in the candy industry if many young girls in their still formative years are not to be exploited to the limit of their endurance during the peak seasons.

3—In the matter of factory sanitation, the need is not so much for new regulations as for the enforcement of those already existing. *The health code requiring a yearly medical examination should be amended, however, to provide for a bi-yearly one.* As has been said before, it is impossible for the limited staff of the Board of Health to enforce sanitation and health codes for 75,000 food-handlers in New York City without the complete co-operation of the employer. The enlightened consumer must bring pressure to bear upon the backward employer, by demanding:

> Complete compliance with all sanitary and health laws.
> Clean, well-lighted factories and clean and healthy workers.

---

When asked if there was anything that the consumer might do to help iron out the peak and slack seasons in the candy industry, the majority of candy manufacturers interviewed answered in the negative. As one man expressed it: "People just naturally eat more candy in winter than in summer. To some extent and with some kinds of candy proper refrigeration makes it possible to shorten the slack season and prepare far in advance for the Christmas rush. But some kinds of candy won't keep more than a few weeks." Another manager declared that such minor holidays as Mother's Day, etc., were helping to lengthen the busy season somewhat. Another stated that the manufacture of such by-products as cocoa, malted chocolate, etc., had cut his after-Christmas lay-off in half.

There is no doubt but that the strict enforcement of the new hours law would do much to stabilize employment by compelling the employer to plan his work more systematically. The study of hours and earnings in five industries made by the Bureau of Women in Industry in 1923 showed quite conclusively that shorter-hour plants had the greatest stability of employment. If a few factories can accomplish comparative stability now, there is no reason why others cannot do the same.

That better wages, reasonable hours and steadier work would do much to raise sanitary standards in the candy industry, cannot be doubted by anyone who has visited a factory where such conditions prevail. The worker who is decently paid and well treated has an interest in her job and a sense of responsibility about her output that would make impossible many of the practices indulged in throughout many factories. The $12 a week girl who knows that she is going to be laid off after Christmas, who is tired and disgusted with fatigue and discomfort, doesn't care what happens to the candy. And it frequently happens.

To the claim that modern, intelligent management and personnel methods cannot be applied successfully in the candy industry due to its seasonal and fluctuating nature, the example of the English industry can be cited as an answer. English confectioners, (such firms as Rowntree's and Cadbury's being notable examples) lead the nation in the development of better working conditions and in the training of their workers.

### The White List.

How may the consumer enforce these demands for better wages, hours and sanitary conditions?

Twenty years ago, when girls in many department stores were earning $5 and $6 a week and were working 10 and 11 hours a day, the Consumers' League began a campaign for better conditions by publishing a White List of those stores which met the requirement of what the League considered fair wages, hours and working conditions. League members and the public were requested to patronize only those firms listed. The League's minimum standards of those days have been surpassed by practically all mercantile establishments today.

That a White List applied to low-standard industrial groups might be equally effective in arousing public interest and in enforcing fair conditions is quite probable. It should be particularly effective in the candy industry which touches the consumer so intimately. A suggested list of *minimum* standards is appended. It should be published only after complete investigation had included factories not covered in the present survey—as well as all those willing to comply with such standards in the future.

That any legitimate industry under intelligent and efficient management can afford to pay its workers a fair wage and surround them with decent working conditions is recognized to-day by management engineers and by a few far-sighted employers. That neither the family nor society should subsidize an industry by helping to support its workers is merely industrial common-sense. The consumer of 1928 has a right to demand that the goods he consumes be made and handled by adequately paid workers under clean and wholesome conditions.

—LILLIAN SYMES.

# SUGGESTED STANDARDS FOR A WHITE LIST IN THE CANDY INDUSTRY.

## General.

1—Compliance with the provisions of the State Labor Law in regard to hours of work and overtime.

*2—A beginning wage of $14 a week.

†3—Provision of seats for all workers in all operations except spread packing. Provision of sufficient seats in spread packing to permit workers to sit at intervals. Permission to use such seats.

## Hygienic Standards.

4—Compliance with the Sanitary Code requiring a "Food Handler's Card" or medical examination for all workers on entry.

5—Medical examination of worker through Board of Health or private or company physician twice a year.

## Sanitary Standards.

6—A clean, well-lighted factory, with clean and sufficient toilets and wash rooms, the latter complying with all provisions of the State Labor Law and Sanitary Codes, to be located in convenient proximity to the work-room.

7—Paper or individual towels, soap and hot water at all times.

8—Enforcement of high standard of personal cleanliness among workers—frequent washing of hands; suppression of finger licking when "sliding cups"; use of aprons over *all* outer clothing.

9—Maintenance of a temperature of at least 64° F. in all departments.

---

* This is not to be interpreted as the League's conception of a fair wage, but rather as a compromise with the realization that no employer can move too far in advance of his competitors.

† Seats for all spread packers are desirable and the type of seats suggested in the text could be ultimately installed. In the meantime, one seat for every three workers (the requirement for mercantile establishments) would permit the worker to take short rests when tired.

*Spread Packing in a Model Factory*     By Ewing Galloway, N. Y.

# THE UNIVERSITY OF MICHIGAN

**DATE DUE**

MAY 0 6

DO NOT REMOVE
OR
MUTILATE CARD

Printed in Poland
by Amazon Fulfillment
Poland Sp. z o.o., Wrocław